PREFERRED COLLECTION

CATHY D. JOHNSON-PENDLETON, AUTHOR

AND

CODY BEASLEY, ARTIST

ABOUT THE AUTHOR

Cathy D. Johnson-Pendleton is a Christian. She attended Cornell College and received a degree in Political Science and History. Mrs. Johnson-Pendleton served in the U.S. Army National Guard.

Mrs. Johnson-Pendleton worked with both the Clinton-Gore and Reagan-Bush campaigns. She has worked as a counselor with children in homeless shelters for families.

ABOUT THE ARTIST

Cody Beasley is a Christian as well as an artist. He also served in the United States Armed Forces as a Combat Engineer.

ACKNOWLEDGMENTS

I would like to thank God for inspiring me to finish this book. This is to all of my friends and family who supported me and encouraged me to continue.

I would like to especially thank my husband, Robert L. Pendleton, Sr. for believing in me. A special thanks goes out to the artist, Edward Taylor for his piece.

CONTENTS

CONTENTS

PART ONE: THOUGHTS TO PONDER

UNCERTAINTY

✳

I don't know what to do,
Tell me, Jesus;
I know not where to go,
Or where my life will be;
Tell me, Jesus
What direction you want me to go?

Let me know where my feet should go?
I don't know what plans you have for my life;
What will my career be?
Tell me, Jesus
Where will my life be?

PLEASE DON'T JUDGE ME

✳

Have you ever seen people who look at you and stare?
They place a label on you that says you're not all there.
The label they put on you says you're no good.
And then they begin to make fun of you.

If you're not doing the things they feel you should do,
Then they begin to scar you.
Some say you're not any good;
oh please, don't make fun of me–
because you don't know when my God is coming down here
to make everything okay.

Because God is Superhuman,
my God can take a bad situation and turn it to a positive thing.
Don't make fun of me.
Because the very ones that you put down, wears a crown
and will end up having everything.

My God does not differentiate between his children.
He makes no distinction among his flock.
So don't laugh,
cause you'll never know when he will turn everything around
upside down.
And you will be confused
for putting me down.

God is superhuman,
so mighty, that He can do anything.
My God is more than sufficient and He loves me.

I STILL WONDER

*

I'm beginning to wonder,
to question my beliefs.
Even though God has answered my prayers,
I still don't believe.
I go back to my Bible
and I wonder is it all true.
But everything in the Bible is truth.
Because when you see how life is,
then you'll know that the Bible is real.
Still, I keep going.

My life seems as though
it has been suppressed;
I wonder should I keep going on,
knowing that I might not have success.
But then when I hear God's words,
it reminds me to go on;
even if it's not the way I want,
I keep going on,
till I see the change in my life.
Till I see the faith that I say I have;
though at times there's disbelief,
yet I keep going on.
Even though I wonder and question my beliefs.
Even though God has answered my prayers,
I still wonder.

GOD I NEED YOU

✳

God, I need you right now!
I feel a little bit down.
My thoughts are scattered
and I can't tell where I'm bound.
It seems as if the blues—
are all I'm able to look to—
I have my mind on everything
that I'm unable to do.
Like the wind
I'm blowing from here and there.
Many times, I don't know where I'm going;
sometimes, I don't even care.

REALIZATION

✴

I got on my knees
the day when I could no longer depend on me.
I, at one time,
truly believed that I was the only one I needed.
Then the Lord Almighty kindly
introduced Himself to me.
He said, I'm God–
I'm the one and only you need.
He suggested, not commanded,
that I come to depend on Him.
He said, did you notice that work sometimes demand that you
take leave?
Jobs and the economy go down.
But He said, dear child,
my hand always lifts up people and blesses them.

THE CREDIT AND THANKS ARE HIS

✳

Let us not forget that the Lord helped us
through;
Remember when we called on Him to get us
out of the blues.
Think of the time when you were hungry,
the Lord God fed you.
What about the time when you did not
have anywhere to lay your head–
He sent someone to aid you.
Think of the time when you did not have
a job,
God put you in the right place to receive that too.
Don't ever forget all that God has done
for you.
Don't steal credit for the things God
has done for you.

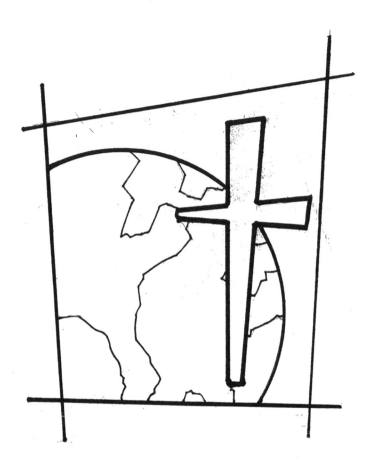

I WANT A MAN LIKE GOD

*

I want a man who always thinks of me first.
I want a man whom I don't have to fear
him looking up another woman's skirt.
I want a man who thinks I'm the most
beautiful.
The man that I choose—
has to be totally dutiful.
Not a man who's looking to use me;
I want a man like you, God,
for if I ask a lot—
he would have the whole world to give.
I want You, Lord,
because I know you really care.

DEAR GOD

✳

Hello, God!
 I'd like to say good morning to You;
 How do You do?
I want to start off by saying
I love You.
I love You because You're You;
You deserve more than the highest praise,
You honestly do.
God, I have You right beside me;
I'm leaning on Your arms;
I lay my head on You,
Just like a baby would be in his mothers' arms.
Safe and truly loved,
But only loved by You.

Dear God,
I'm writing You to say thank You;
It's going to always be me and just You;
I'm actually complacent with the love of you.

I'LL TELL MY FATHER

✳

You're going to have to answer to my
Father.
You keep treating me mean,
Stepping and walking all over me;
You're going to have to answer to my
Father
The mighty one in heaven.
Stomping on me,
Mistreating me,
Jealous of me,
I'm beginning to think that you don't even
like me.
For a dog, if you don't like him, you'll
leave him alone
Or he will bite you.
With me you continue to oppress me,
Trying very hard to suppress me.
If you continue on
I'm going to pray to the Almighty One
And ask and plead with Him
To get you off of me.

FOCUS

✳

I know it seems as though
  The rich are down here having a ball,
  Rich, and full of material blessings,
parties and balls.
But they don't have it all
Because the world down here,
Is a short time for everybody.
Heaven should be the aim for all.
Heaven is eternity;

So don't envy the rich and famous at all.
Because Heaven and God are all that
matters in life, at all.

STINGY ME

✷

Stingy as I can be.
With the money God has given me,
Trying to find a way to
Give God $2 instead of $3.
Dislike paying my tithes;
Why should I give God anything–
If I don't give it to Him,
I can spend it for a diamond ring.
I say that God is asking me for money
unnecessarily.
When my health has gone to the pits,
I go to God putting my bids in–
Pleading for mercy and His perfect hands
to heal me.
When I cannot pay my bills,
I ask God for a couple of thousand
to pay the rent and other things.
How ironic that I cannot dig into my
pockets to give God 10 percent.

29

GO TO YOU

✳

God, when I realized
That it was You
That I should ask for food;
When my feet hurt,
I went to You, so that you could make a way
to buy me some shoes;
My credit was so bad
I needed divine intervention
To let my rental application go through,
If I had known better
In the past, I wouldn't have gone to others,
instead of You.
God, you get things done;
You get them done better than others do.

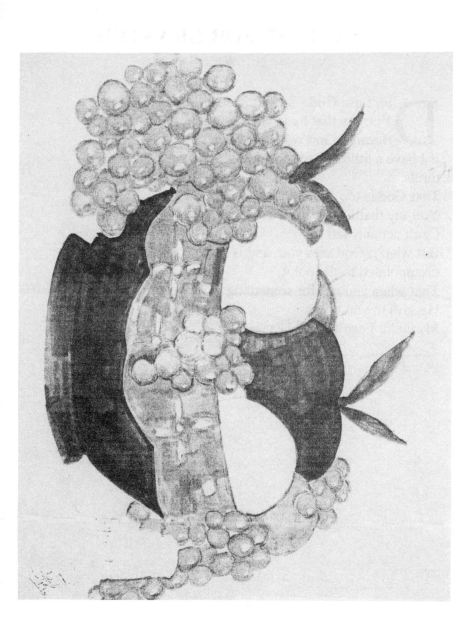

TAKE ME FOR GRANTED

✳

Don't use God.
You say that I can sin
Because God will forgive me;
If I have a little sex and get a few
thrills,
That God is too far to hear me.
You say that a little bit of drugs,
Can't actually kill me.
But what if God sees you, and is
disappointed to the point,
That when you ask for something in prayer,
He says to you;
My child, I can't really hear you.

LOOKING WITHIN

✳

Will we see our oppressor in heaven or hell?
You decide where you will be.
We try to copy-cat them;
Only because we feel they are right.
God alone determines whether we belong in
heaven or hell.
So God's the one we need to take heed of
and to really care for;
Let's open our hearts to the Lord Jesus,
Allow Him to pry the filth out of our
hearts;
We need to clean up our act
and renew our minds.

GOD DESERVES THE SAME

*

If you can stay up
All night long,
Looking at TV and hanging out,
when God wakes you
for a conversation and a good talk,
do not delay, give God His way.
He wants to talk with you
About the foolishness, and the trashy
thoughts–
that plague you
like windy dust.
When you wake up at three o'clock in the morning,
God says, this is a good time
to fill your head,
to remove the junk food stuff that others
have put in.
To clear your mind of negative thinking,
road blocks and man-made dead ends.

IF GOD WAS HUMAN

✳

What if God was like us—
  Had human tendencies and all the rest of
  that stuff.
What if He didn't forgive us like we so
many times don't forgive one another—
When someone uses us, again and again,
We fight back and decide not to give in.

We as humans, most of the time will not
allow others
to abuse us, use us, lie to or deceive us.
We say we will never let it happen again.
Now let's suppose God were like this—
if God had human tendencies—
how or where would we be?

DOWN THE ROAD, NOT ALONE

✳

Do you ever feel lonely?
Do you feel like you're alone?
Traveling down a paved road,
So alone by yourself.
Have you wondered on those trips you took to nowhere.
Trying to find peace of mind;
Wanting, yet hoping, to be there with someone.

Can you remember the very first time
when you felt a dark night?
At first, you could not understand why you did not see.
That you weren't alone–
but you felt it anyhow.

So, you drove a little further down the road and a bright
glare came to you.
That's when you found, that you weren't alone you see.
This name called Jesus;
He said come to me and you'll be in peace;
Just follow me.

You continued to drive down the lonely road;
and thought, you were all alone.
The cracks in the road were rough, then you turned the corner
Only to go up hill;
You shifted gears;
The end of the road came near,
There was a sign saying, don't go here.
At the end of your road;
Crying–not knowing what to do.
So alone.

A voice said, come to Me,
you'll be at peace;
I'm your friend to the end.

Saying: I was with you when the cracks in the road
appeared;
Then you went up hill and I had to shift your gears;
I was there when you cried that you were all alone
out there;
I was there with you when you thought no one cared;
I'll say again: Give your life to Me;
Follow me so you can be free;

Come to Me, cause I'll never leave you;
You'll never be alone cause Jesus will be right there;
He says: follow Me;
there will be no trips any more
to nowhere.

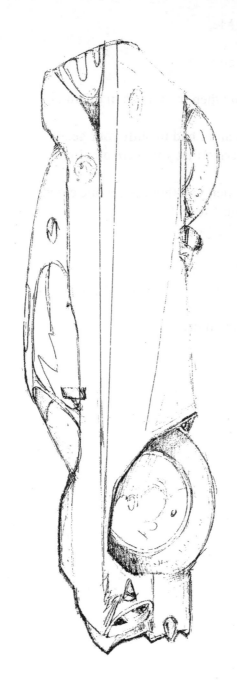

PART TWO: DAILY CONCERNS

WORLDLY PASSIONS

✳

Jesus, I'm so caught up in the flesh,
   that I don't know which problem to address.
   All I want to do is fulfill the flesh.
 I would like to put certain worldly desires behind;
Absorbed in the benefits of living down here,
Concerned with all the earthly possessions.
God, please put me in check.

54

WAR IN NORTH AMERICA

✳

Instead of fighting and having wars in other
peoples' countries.
We could have the US Army policing the ghetto areas.
In high crime cities of North America,
the Army and Marines could police the metropolitan areas.
The National Guard could take over the heavy drug traffic areas,
wipe out the drug dealers and rehabilitate the addicts.
Overtake the neighborhoods.
War should be fought here in North America.

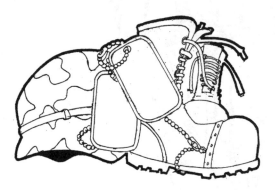

THE WAY IT IS

✳

Sometimes people can't help the way they come out,
Who they are born of,
Or where they have been.
People can't help it if they are rich or poor.
Nor, if they tend to give into their weaknesses.
Sometimes people can't help the way they turn out.

49

SPEAK

✳

People want to speak–
  but the frown on many faces
  keeps a hello from going forth.
People may want to say, hello!
But along comes an unhappy disposition
to turn someone around.

SPEAK!

SOCIETY'S NOT BOTHERED

✳

What's going on in the inner cities?
The mayors, politicians and congressional
leaders aren't doing anything for the poor people.
The poor are left slipping through the cracks.
The system has forgotten them,
Left them in polluted and drug infested areas with the rats.
People hang out on the corner–shooting dice.
Sluggards, muggers and robbers, drug pushers
who intimidate the good.

JEALOUSY BREEDS OPPRESSION

✳

Whether one has material blessings
or is of a certain color–
this makes a person,
put the heat down on his brother.
Mainly because someone thinks that someone else
has something "so-called" over another.
One person doesn't necessarily have to be "better" than
the other,
he or she just perceives that he or she has
more in life than the other.

LAZY MAN

＊

A man lives with this woman,
of course she works.
He on the other hand–
Would not lift up dirt.
She washes his shirts,
Stained and filthy with dirt,
While all he does
Is complain of frustrations and hurts.
She prepares his meals,
Laboring all day long
For this lazy, dead-beat and bum.

PAINS OF DISTINCTION

✳

Sorrow and pain
are not the same.
Pain you feel,
sorrow you borrow,
from the thoughts of yesterday, today or tomorrow.
Pain aches.
You need a pill to get rid of the aches.
Medicine cannot get rid of sorrow;
Pains of distinction of distorted sorrows.

PERCEPTION

❋

Perceptions are formed about the people around us;
We look at a person and conjure up ideas
about them in our own image.
There's a madness about it all.
As we try to form opinions about other people;
Professors read poetry to try to figure out what an
author is writing all about.
In turn, people look at one another
to see what they are made of.
A mere perception is all that will be seen.

STRUGGLE TO SURVIVE
✳

Each day is a battle.
The battle could be at home with your spouse,
or with your children.
The battle could be at work between employer and employee.
Survival isn't necessarily a physical fight to maintain existence.
A struggle to survive could be one in the mind.

ELITE

✳

Elite class of people,
    What are you doing to the masses of people?
    You take away food from hungry mouths;
because of your greed, they are devoured.
Elite class of people,
You leave the little ones like me,
devastated and incomplete.
Making a bare living,
with only enough for food to eat.

DEAR LANDLORD

✳

Landlord, you take most of my money from me.
After a hard day's work,
You leave me with one-fourth of my
paycheck–substantially decreased.
You force me to live my life always on the brink;
landlord, you could care less about me.

DEAR LANDLORD

PART THREE:
SCRATCHING THE SURFACE

YOU SHOT YOUR FRIEND

*

If you live your life in the fast lane
Focusing only on money, power and fame.
Desiring to make a fast buck,
Foresight you need to gain.
Have a keen sense of your future,
As far as the outcome.
Think man, when you kill
who do you think you're killing?
Certainly not your enemy–
you just shot your friend dead.
The reason you can't determine your friend from your foe.
Is that the "man" has confused you utterly, so.

LOVE

✳

Oh, my black people.
Do you know who you are?
You could soar the highest mountain.

You were created in the image of God.
God looks like you.
Please, don't destroy the person whom God created.
You could move mountains my Black brother,
when you start sticking together
instead of beating up on one another.

LOVE!

TOGETHERNESS

*

Let's get it together my black brothers,
in the US and across the world.
Stop and think, why would you kill your own brother?

Nothing is worth it.
Whether it be land or gold.
For if you shorten the black lineage,
The master dream will not unfold.

You have a future, Black and handsome brother.
To show the world,
that you are a "bad" people of color.

IT'S MY LIFE

✳

To inflict your values on me
　　Would imply that I care about the same things in life that
　　you do.
You have your life, and I have mine.
To think that my desires in life replicate yours,
is presumptuous.
The level where I've reached is much too deep.

It's my life
to enjoy, to laugh and to love.

RACISM

✳

Trying to love my brother,
Is not an easy thing to do.
My brother hates me;
when he looks at my color--he judges me;
but, that's another challenge to overcome.

My brother, though he doesn't realize he is,
treats me with disdain.
On the job, he often overlooks me.
God will help me over that wall.

FACES OF PAIN

*

Crying out.
    Each day I cry.
    Some hearts are ripped apart,
Hollering to let all the pain out.
Everything is tumbling down.

Do you know why some people look mean?
Someone has taken away their dreams.
Their goals are gone,
that's why you see pain in their eyes.
Unable to express what they feel inside.
Creativity is lost and never found.
That's why you see pain in my peoples eyes.

DISCRIMINATION

✳

Discriminated against?
Sure you've been.
Tired of being treated like a second class citizen?
Judged by the color of your skin.
Told what you can do in order to achieve?
Tired of this whole scene.
You want and desire the same things;
as other prospering human beings.

WHO CARES

✳

When people think you're nice,
they try your patience.
Some people think you need them.
They just don't know,
That you are not concerned.

So what, if they don't care for you.
If they think that you are pressed,
they are sadly mistaken.
My strength comes from where they don't know.
So, I won't acknowledge them,
That's the way it goes.

BULLIES

✳

They are the ones who drop out of school,
act like hoodlums, and who the teachers boo;
They are the ones who are not really cool;
some bullies are dropouts,
since they cop out of life too.

Some are on drugs heavily.
A few are not quite educated,
that's why the bullies behave as they do.
Cutting up, like fools in schools.

SOMETHING BETTER

❉

I want a change in my situation;
Don't want to make a bare living–just to keep me afloat.

I want to be able to move from the ghetto scene;
don't want to get caught up in the cross fire of things;
I need a breakthrough.

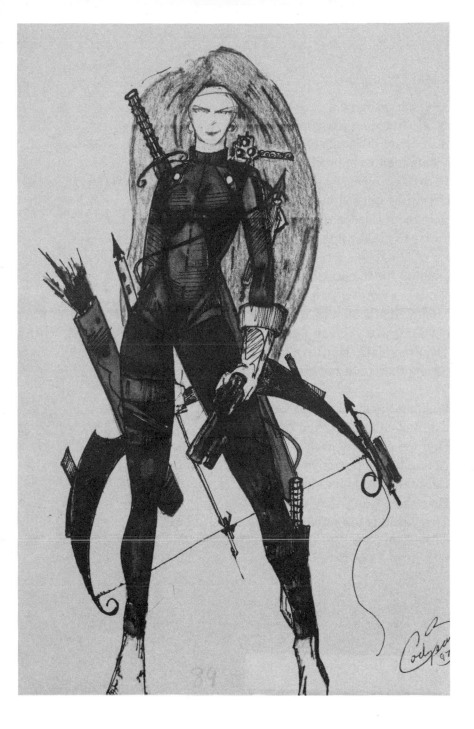

PAIN

*

Pain, pain, pain
  My God, please take it away.
  Drug boys taking over this world.
Killing their own brothers upon this earth.

Have they gone stone mad?
Help them Lord, they are in pain.
Please God take it away.

Fighting for the dollar,
When it's not worth it.
Money, that's all it is, money,
in your grave you can't take it with you.
They're killing their own people of color.
Saying that's not my brother.

Walking by, in this mean world,
won't even look at their own brother.
Don't even know, if they're distant cousins.
Acting like hypo active fools.
Cause they're killing one another.
Help them Lord, they're in pain.
This world is too much for drug boys to bear.
They're in pain.

CITY STREETS

✳

Sirens going off in the city streets;
the sounds of gun fire you can hear.
You know that the drug dealers are fighting,
so near, in the area where you live.
But you can't do any better.
Having to live in a war zone
is life threatening.
So, you pray to God
that nothing bad happens.

JUNGLE CITY

✳

L iving in the city where crime is so heavy,
Hoping that you don't get hit by one of
those flying bullets.
Innocent people dying and suffering,
not really having anything to do with the problems.
Not enough police or politicians to handle the thing;
no control of the universe by man you see.

HANG IN THERE--PEOPLE OF POVERTY

✳

Riding on the bus;
walking down the streets,
you see people living in poverty.
Folks hanging out on the corner,
shooting the breeze.
Children looking as if they lack something.
Teenagers strolling with nothing to do,
adults carrying the look–
as if to say, I've been there too.

All jammed up in substandard project housing.
Hold on people of poverty–
cause there will be a day when the Lord will call you.

BLACK MEN: WAKE UP!

✳

Standing on the corner
   Trying to look cool.
   Is not in, black men, you need to be schooled;
Putting a bottle up to your mouth,
smoking crack is not popular, or where it's at.
Wearing gold, shining bright,
does nothing for your personality;
nor does it make you more enlightened.

Do you think the wearing of gold portrays to others
that you have a lot?
When you impress the ladies,
by buying very expensive Mercedes.
What you believe is the in-thing to do,
is to have five or six ladies, dangling.
Never actually realizing,
you could end up acting crazy.

Black men, you especially have to wake up from the long
nightmare you've been in.

Come out of the jails;
Don't give satan what he wants.
For you to be lost and distraught.

OPPRESSION

✳

No one can depress me.
What others think of me will not penetrate
my attitude towards myself.
I can neither be oppressed or depressed,
by the finger or by the touch of man.
Clutching to burst my bubble.

The reason I'm so mighty,
and can keep any man from crushing me,
is Jesus.
He has given me the power to fight off the enemy.

THE CITY'S EXPENSES

✴

Have you seen the many parking attendants,
Riding around in search for a car to ticket?
While the city has other more pressing problems,
for instance, people robbing and folks getting mugged.
The city would rather hire someone to tow and ticket our cars.

Our city's priorities are not quite in order,
Or else there would be more cops arresting others.
Crime would drop significantly.
The city could hire more policemen.
If true law were in order.

Which are the lesser of the two evils?
A citizen getting shot, or a car being ticketed?

A DIFFERENT COLOR

※

If you don't want to act right
that's okay with me.
I ain't got to have a black man you see.

It makes no difference about the color
Girlfriend, you had better get you another lover.
He could be White, Spanish, or Chinese,
Indian, African, or Mexican.
But you had better get one that's right for you.

When you stick within your own race
you limit yourself.
Then you wind up taking a bunch of stuff,
because you are too afraid to go outside your race.

Girlfriend you had better get you another lover
White, Spanish, or Chinese,
Indian, African, or Mexican,
it shouldn't matter what he is.